EASY
IMPROVEMENTS

your kitchen

EASY HOME IMPROVEMENTS

your kitchen

STEWART WALTON

LEBHAR-FRIEDMAN BOOKS

New York • Chicago • Los Angeles • London • Paris • Tokyo

Lebhar-Friedman Books
425 Park Avenue
New York, NY 10022

First U.S. edition published 2000 by Lebhar-Friedman Books
Copyright © 2000 Marshall Editions Ltd., London U. K.

Published by Lebhar-Friedman Books
Lebhar-Friedman Books is a company of Lebhar-Friedman, Inc.

Originated in Singapore by Pica.
Printed and bound in China by Excel Printing.

Library of Congress Cataloging-In-Publication Data:
Walton, Stewart.
  Your kitchen / Stewart Walton.
    p. cm.
  ISBN 0-86730-791-9 (alk. paper)
   1. Kitchens--Remodeling--Amateurs' manuals. I. Title.

TH4816.3.K58 W35 2000
643'.4--dc21   00-021811

Project Editor Ian Kearey

Designed by Paul Griffin

Photographer Alistair Hughes

Managing Editor Antonia Cunningham

Managing Art Editor Patrick Carpenter

Editorial Director Ellen Dupont

Art Director Dave Goodman

Editorial Coordinator Ros Highstead

Production Amanda Mackie

Indexer Jill Dormon

Front cover photography: **Robert Harding Picture Library**
back cover: **Alistair Hughes**

Visit our Web site at lfbooks.com

Note

contents

introduction

As well as being the place where we prepare and eat many of our meals, any kitchen bigger than a closet tends to be a meeting place and a center for a house. In times gone by, the kitchen stove might have been the only form of semi-permanent warmth, and even in these days of double glazing and central heating, something of that sense of family and community persists. Giving your kitchen an imaginative makeover means that your hard work and creative input will be seen and appreciated by both residents and visitors alike.

In this book, I designed the projects to be accessible to as wide a range of people as possible. In the introduction to each set of step-by step photographs and text, the project is given a skill rating of Beginner, Intermediate, or Advanced. Of course, to give just one example, someone with experience in woodworking, for whom laying floorboards poses no problem, may find designing and making a stencil less easy, and the reverse will be true for a practiced paint-finish decorator.

The important thing is to look at all the stages of each project before you tackle it and, above all, take your time—the times given in the introductory section for the projects assume you have all the materials and tools on hand and can work uninterruptedly until you have finished. The additional work needed to finish a project—treating wood, applying protection, painting, and varnishing—are not included in the times, nor are drying times for glue, wood putty, and finishes.

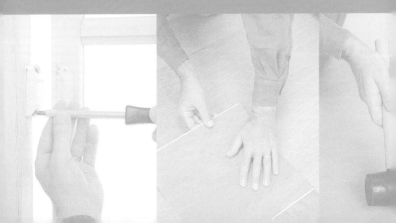

For the larger-scale projects—laying laminated floating floors or stencilling all four walls in three colors—I have included a rough guide to how long you can expect to take on the marking out and preparation; once this is done, the time will depend on the area to be covered and the materials you use.

Note that the dimensions given in the Materials lists are for the finished size of each component; you can adapt projects such as the herb window box or plate rack to fit your own requirements. If you intend to change the size radically, you may have to reconsider the width and depth you use for each component, both for strength and proportions.

When it comes to tools, the golden rule is that you get what you pay for. Inexpensive tools may seem a bargain, but their drawbacks can range from measuring inaccurately to falling apart while working—and for power tools, this can lead to injury or worse. Make a careful check on secondhand tools, and inspect the condition of the wiring in electrical tools.

Don't let these dire warnings put you off. If you follow the manufacturer's instructions, and wear protective clothing where necessary, you should not have a problem. Good tools do cost, so build up your tool kit as and when you can; and to save spending money on equipment that may only be used once or twice, most rental stores hire out large and small power tools by the day or weekend.

I hope you get enjoyment and a sense of having achieved something worthwhile out of these projects.

Stewart Walton

chapter 1
walls

tiling a **splashback**

A splashback surface doesn't just have to be useful—surrounding it with a frame of painted flat wood or a molding profile means you can turn it into a kitchen "feature" as well. Small tiles are best, because you can make up a large or small area without needing to cut them; we used 4 x 4 in. tiles.

Materials

Ceramic wall tiles • ½ x ¾ in. softwood or molding • Tile adhesive • Grout • Wall-tile spacers • PVA (white) glue • Brads • Wood putty • Paint

Tools

Miter saw • Utility knife • Adhesive spreader • Hammer • Center punch • Grout shaper • Paintbrush • Abrasive paper • Carpenter's level • Square • Flexible grout spreader or sponge

Skill level

Intermediate

Time

2–3 hours

Easy home improvements

1 Decide how large an area of wall you want to cover,
then lay out the appropriate number of tiles on a clean,
flat surface, placing X-shape wall-tile spacers in all the
inner spaces. Remember that the greater number of
spacers you need to use, the larger the area will be.

2 Because there will be a gap for grout all around
between the tiles and the frame, you need to place cut
spacers on the corners and outer spaces. Using a
sharp blade in a utility knife, carefully trim the spacers
for the corners to an "L" shape, and those for the
edges to a "T" shape. Insert the spacers, close the tiles
to fit exactly, and check that they are square.

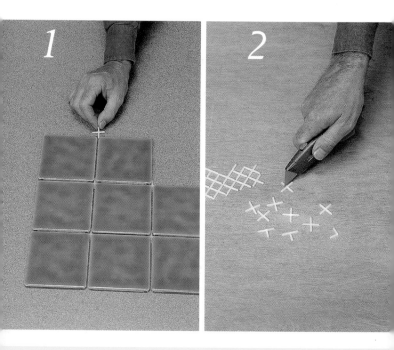

3 Measure the distance between the two top corner spacers, and transfer it to the flat softwood or profiled molding. The marks are the inside of the 45-degree miters on the wood. Cut the wood using a miter saw set to 45 degrees, and sand the cut ends.

4 Place the wood in position against the spacers along the top of the tiles. If it is accurate, mark it as the top piece, move it aside, then repeat step 3 for the three remaining pieces, each time checking the fit of the miter joint against the others. Fit the frame together, and check that it is square.

Helpful hints

Packs of wall-tile spacers are available from hardware or decorating stores. When cutting them into L or T shapes for this project, it is a good idea to make 50 percent more than you intend to use.

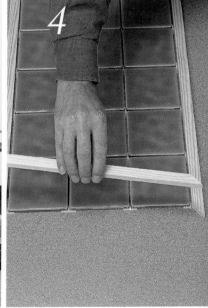

5 Place the bottom frame piece in position on the work surface and wall, and mark its ends. Apply a few blobs of PVA (white) glue to the back, then nail it in position using brads. Wipe off any excess glue with a clean, damp cloth.

6 Place one of the vertical pieces of wood against the miter of the bottom piece, and check it with a square. Mark its exact position, then apply glue and nail in the piece as in step 5. If you like, you can use the square or a carpenter's level to keep the position absolutely accurate. Repeat for the other vertical piece, and then finish with the top strip of wood.

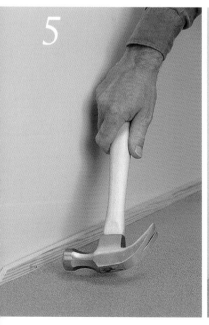
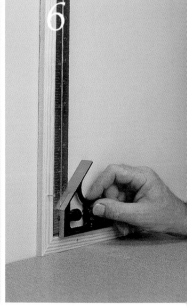

7 Using a center punch and hammer, punch all the heads of the brads just below the surface of the wood. Apply quick-drying wood putty to the brad holes and to any gaps in the mitered corners of the frame, following the manufacturer's instructions. Allow to dry.

8 Many tile adhesives are supplied with a plastic applicator/spreader, or they are sold separately. Apply the adhesive as directed—up to about 3 sq. ft. is the standard, but areas up to 4½ sq. ft. can be done in one go—and spread the grooves to get an even, ridged surface. Take your time on this, and don't try to rush it.

9 Start by tiling the bottom row. Place one of the L-shape corner spacers in position, then add the corner tile, giving it a little wiggle in the adhesive to make sure it grips. Place the T-shape spacers in position along the bottom and side, add the next bottom tile, and repeat, adding the upper-edge, X-shape spacers as you go.

10 Work along each row, making sure the tiles and spacers fit together accurately, and removing any excess blobs of adhesive that prevent a good fit. After the last tile and spacers are fitted, allow the adhesive to dry completely—this usually takes about 24 hours. Remove any adhesive that has strayed onto the tile or frame surfaces.

11 Sand the wood putty on the nail holes and mitered corners, clear away the dust, and paint the wood as required. We used the same color as the wall to allow the tiles to stand out. When the paint is dry, apply grout liberally to the gaps between the tiles, and the tiles and frame, and use a flexible spreader or clean, damp sponge to fill the gaps.

12 Clean off grout from the tile surfaces and frame, then use a round-end grout shaper to give a profile to the grout—you can buy shapers, but it is just as easy to shape a piece of wood, or find wood or metal with the desired profile. Clean up the grout, and allow to dry. Polish the ceramic tiles with a soft, dry cloth.

stencilling
a wall

Stencilling is a long-established technique for adding color to your walls without having to go over the whole surface. You can apply as many or as few stencils as you like and use one or more colors. In fact the possibilities are limitless—you can stencil on painted furniture, doors, and even wooden floors. Easy though the technique may seem, don't be tempted to skimp on materials: always use proper stencil cards and stencil brushes, available from art-supply stores. The stencil used here, and some other designs for inspiration, are shown on pp 106–109.

Materials
Stencil card • Water-base paint (acrylic) • Stencil brush

Tools
Hobby knife or scalpel • Low-tack spray adhesive • Low-tack adhesive tape • White ceramic plate • Clean rag or absorbent kitchen paper

Skill level
Intermediate

Time
15–30 minutes to cut stencil; 15–30 minutes to apply two colors

Easy home improvements

1. When you have copied or drawn your stencil pattern to the right size for your requirements, cut it to the same size and shape as a piece of stencil card. Apply low-tack spray adhesive to one or both surfaces (according to the manufacturer's instructions), and press the pattern onto the card, smoothing from the center outward. Make sure there are no air bubbles trapped between the pattern and the card.

2. Allow the adhesive to dry, then place the card on a piece of scrap plywood or a cutting mat. Cut out the pattern through the paper and the stencil card using a sharp hobby knife or scalpel.

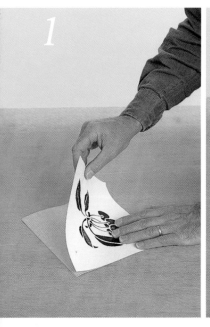

3 Remove the paper template from the stencil card, working slowly and carefully. Check the card and use the hobby knife to tidy up any loose or ragged edges.

4 Squeeze out some acrylic or other water-based paint onto a clean, dry, white ceramic plate. Having all the colors ready on the plate means you can move quickly from one to another. Dab the stencil brush into the first color, making sure the ends of all the bristles are covered. Don't overload the brush.

Helpful hints

As well as applying a stencil on its own, you can also add fine details or embellishments using water-based paints and a fine artist's brush.

5 The stencil brush must be almost dry, so remove all but the last traces of paint with a clean rag or absorbent kitchen paper. Test the brush on a piece of scrap paper and repeat until you are satisfied.

6 Place the stencil card in position on the wall and use low-tack tape to fix it there. For the purposes of this demonstration, only one card is being used; if you intend to paint over a large surface, consider making up a number of stencils and fixing them at equal distances along the wall surface.

7 Apply the paint by dabbing or wiping the brush through the cutouts in the stencil card. For a three-dimensional effect, add more paint to certain areas to darken them—don't try to do this by putting more paint on the brush, but apply more with the almost-dry bristles.

8 Allow the first color to dry completely—because it is applied so dry, this does not take long—then add the second color. To give a rounded, three-dimensional effect to the shapes, wipe the brush near the edge of the stencil before dabbing the rest on lightly. Allow to dry before adding any further colors. When all the colors are dry, carefully remove the card.

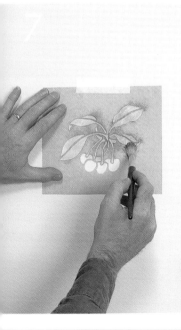

rag-rolling
a wall

With its random, broken-color effect, rag-rolling is a stylish way of covering a wall—in addition, it can be used to distract the eye from an uneven wall surface. Once you have applied a solid-color base coat, time is of the essence, and you need two people: one to apply the glaze coat, and one to dab it off with the cloth.

Materials

Color water-based paint • Glaze • Alkyd paint for base coat

Tools

Paintbrushes • Paint buckets • Low-tack masking tape • Soft, dry, lint-free cloth

Skill level

Beginner

Time

10–15 minutes per 2 sq. yd.

1 Thoroughly clean and degrease the wall surface using a proprietary wall cleaner. Brush on two coats of alkyd, latex, or "vinyl silk" paint, aiming for a smooth, fully covered surface, and allow to dry completely.

2 Cut low-tack masking tape into strips and use these to cover woodwork along the walls—dado rails, moldings, baseboards, door and window frames, and so on. Press down firmly, particularly at the meeting point of the woodwork and wall.

Helpful hints

All paintbrushes must be absolutely clean and dry before applying glaze. If you are in any doubt, wash and dry them thoroughly again.

3 Check on the container how much glaze is needed for the area you want to cover, then pour more than this into a clean paint bucket. Add a very little amount of water-based color paint to this, stir thoroughly, and test the mixture out on an area you don't mind painting over or a piece of scrap wood painted with the base color. Make more tinted glaze than you need because it is almost impossible to exactly reproduce a color/glaze mix.

4 To achieve an even, smooth glaze surface over the wall, load the paintbrush, squeeze out the excess against the paint-bucket side, and apply light, regular patches of glaze at regular intervals along the wall. Work over about 2 sq. yd. at a time.

5 Brush out each of the patches and work them together by painting in all directions until you have a smooth, even coat of colored glaze. Make sure you work the glaze well into corners and where the wall meets the masking tape.

6 Take a clean, dry, soft, lint-free cloth and scrunch it into one hand until it is a cauliflower or cabbage shape. The "rolling" surface must have a similar profile to that in the photograph, but must not be too loose or too tight—experience will tell you what works best for you.

Helpful hints

Before starting any painting, glazing, or varnishing project, check the condition of your brushes. Stopping to pick loose bristles off a surface can ruin your concentration, so be careful not to use any old brushes.

7 Dab the rag onto the glaze and rotate it a little to pick up part of the glaze. Work gently, because too much pressure will create too contrasted an effect, and don't pull the rag across the glaze. Continue across the entire glazed area, changing the face of the rag if it becomes too loaded with glaze, and paying special attention to corners and meeting points.

8 If any glaze is inadvertently applied where it shouldn't be, wipe it off immediately with a damp cloth. When finished, allow the glaze to dry completely—check the manufacturer's instructions on the container for the time, which can be up to 24 hours. Remove the masking tape carefully.

color-washing
a wall

Color-washing is a popular way of breaking up and softening solid-color paint, and the potential combinations of a base color and two different color washes are endless. The method is quite easy to learn—the skill lies in building up a rhythm in your brushstrokes and applying just the right amount of diluted paint. The same technique can also be used with glaze, and can be applied to woodwork and furniture.

Materials
Color alkyd paint • White alkyd paint • Water

Tools
Paintbrushes • Paint buckets • Low-tack masking tape

Skill level
Beginner

Time
15–20 minutes per 4–5 sq. yd.

Prepare the walls and cover the woodwork as for rag-rolling (see p. 26). Measure color alkyd paint into a paint bucket, and dilute it with tap water in a mixture of one part paint with two parts water. Mix thoroughly.

Dip a paintbrush into the mixture, squeeze off excess paint against the bucket side, and then brush the diluted mixture onto the wall. Brush in all directions, working steadily but quickly—the paint will dry quite fast.

Helpful hints

If you decide to mix your own colors, it is essential to either make notes on the exact proportions used, or to make much more than you will need. Cover the paint bucket with plastic film to keep it from setting overnight.

3 Stand back regularly and look at the area you have been working on. Don't worry if the covering appears patchy, but make sure you do cover as much as you wish. Allow this coat to dry completely, and wash out the paint bucket and paintbrush thoroughly.

4 Make up a diluted mixture of one part white alkyd paint with three parts water. To reduce the brilliance of the white, add a very little amount of the color paint a tiny bit at a time. Load a dry brush very sparingly with this mix, squeeze out any excess against the side, then brush on very lightly in all directions as before. Use up all the paint on the brush before reloading it.

chapter 2
floors

laying vinyl
floor tiles

Vinyl tiles are an easy, attractive way to cover a floor area, particularly if you have a small kitchen where it might be difficult to position and mark sheet vinyl—in addition, if one is marked or damaged, replacing it is no problem. We used self-adhesive tiles for speed and convenience, and because they have an irregular pattern, we laid them in a checkerboard formation.

Materials
Self-adhesive vinyl floor tiles • Floor cleaner • Gloss-finish floor polish

Tools
Chalk string • Utility knife • Straightedge • Square • Fine-point felt-tip pen

Skill level
Beginner/Intermediate

Time
2–3 hours per 3 sq. yd.

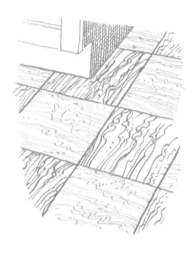

1 Level the floor with hardboard, if necessary. Measure both end walls, not including recesses or bays, and find the mid-point of each. Tap in a brad at these points and stretch a chalk string between them, then snap the string to give a straight chalk line across the room.

2 Mark the center of the line, use a square to draw a right angle, then repeat the process with the brads and chalk string along this second line. Working outward from the center point, lay a line of tiles in both directions along one chalk mark.

Helpful hints

New hardboard or plywood flooring should be laid rough-side up and be treated with an appropriate sealant. Follow the manufacturer's instructions when applying, and allow the sealant to dry before laying out and fitting the tiles.

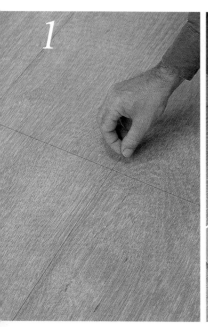

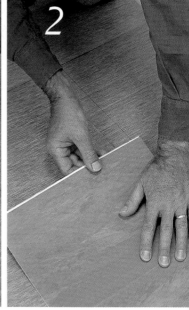

3 When you reach the ends of the line before the walls, place the last tile over the next one, slide it to the wall, and mark or measure the overlap. Repeat at the other end. If the measurements are unequal, move the whole line of tiles over until you have an even border, then snap another chalk line, as in step 1, to replace the first one.

4 Repeat step 3 for the chalk line at right angles, and adjust accordingly. When you are satisfied, sweep or vacuum the floor thoroughly. Even though you do not need to start with the quarter of the room farthest from the door, because there is no adhesive or grout to dry, it is good practice to follow this convention. Peel the backing from the first tile.

5 Lay the tile at the center point where the two chalk lines converge. Press it down gently, working from the center outward across the whole surface, and finish by running your hand around the edge. Continue filling the quarter with whole tiles, making sure the floor surface is clean before you lay each tile.

6 To achieve an accurate fit to the baseboard or kitchen units, position a single tile exactly over the last fixed one, then place another tile on top of this, butting up to the baseboard—trim off any stray backing first. Use a fine-point, felt-tip pen to mark the first tile along the overlap of the two tiles.

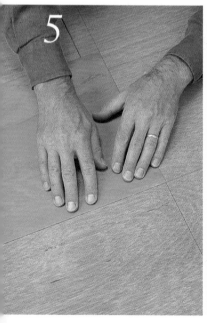

7 Place the marked tile on a scrap piece of hardboard or plywood, and cut along the line with a utility knife and straightedge. Peel off the backing, lay the cut edge against the baseboard, and press into position as in step 5. Continue along the border in this way.

8 Go over the whole floor area as shown in steps 5–7, then sweep or vacuum away any dirt and dust. Clean the tiles using a proprietary vinyl floor cleaner, rinse (if required), and allow to dry. Apply gloss-finish floor polish according to the manufacturer's instructions— usually two coats—and allow to dry completely.

Helpful hints

Before laying the tiles on hardboard or plywood, use a center punch and hammer to punch all nail heads below the floor surface, otherwise they can work their way through the vinyl and damage it through regular wear.

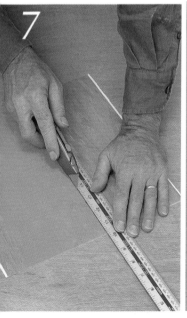

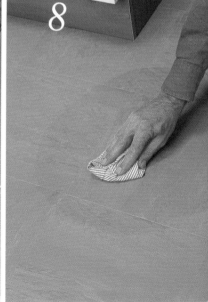

laying a floating
laminated floor

Laminated floorboards are available in a range of thicknesses, from ⅜ in. to ¾ in., and in a great variety of finishes using thin coverings of attractive hardwoods. The tongue-and-groove edges mean that you can butt them up together neatly, and fitting a quadrant hardwood molding around the edges of the floorboards adds a nice touch. Don't skimp on the protective part of this project—like all woods, these floorboards are susceptible to heat, cold, and above all, dampness.

Materials

⅝-in plywood • ½-in laminated floorboards • ¾-in quadrant molding • Polyethylene sheets • Thin styrofoam rolls • 1-in brass brads • 1-in veneer pins

Tools

Crosscut saw • Jigsaw • Backsaw • Miter saw • Hammer • Tongue-and-groove protector or scrap wood • Combination square • Straightedge • Pencil • PVA (white) glue • Center punch • Scissors • Utility knife • Plastic floor spacers • Wood putty • Abrasive paper

Skill level

Intermediate/Advanced

Time

Upward of 4 hours, depending on size of floor

1 The floor surface must be clean, dry, and level before starting. With a wooden floor, use a center punch to push down all protruding nails, staples, and so on below the floor surface. Cut and fit a ⅝-in. plywood surface with irregular, stepped meeting points to ensure a solid base. Place the plywood in position and nail it in with brass brads. Center-punch the brad heads as in the original flooring.

2 To make an effective damp-proof membrane below the laminated floor strips, measure thin polyethylene sheets to fit over the plywood and cut them with scissors or a utility knife. These should overlap by 4–5 in. at each meeting point. Make sure the polyethylene is not damaged before laying it.

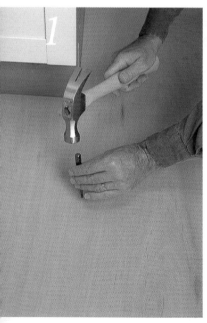

3 To protect the polyethylene, and to make a sub-surface
for the flooring, roll out a layer of thin styrofoam over
it. The strips of styrofoam should cover the meeting
points in the polyethylene, and each piece should be
butted up to the next one, not overlapping. Trim the
styrofoam with scissors or a utility knife, making sure
you are completely accurate at the corners.

4 Start laying the laminated boards in one corner and
move along a square, straight wall with the tongue
facing outward. Because the wood will expand after it
has been fitted (see p. 47), some manufacturers sup-
ply plastic spacers, graded by width—here, ⅛ in.— to
be fitted against the edges around the room. You can
also buy spacers separately from hardware stores.

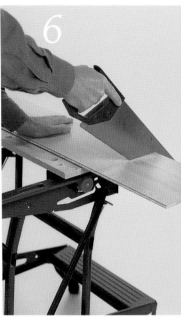

When you get to the end of one line and have to cut a length of board to fit against the adjacent surface, reverse the next board so that its tongue will fit the groove in the laid one. Butt it up to the end and use a combination square to mark across it.

Remove the end board and cut it to length with a fine-tooth crosscut saw or jigsaw. The depth of the tongue at the wall end should compensate for the spacer, although it is a good idea to lay one anyway. Apply glue to the tongue and put it in position in the groove. Nail the completed line in place using brass brads; for neatness, mark out the positions of the brads before nailing, rather than doing it by eye alone.

7 A full length of the next line of laminated boards should be adjacent to the cut end of the first one. Apply PVA (white) glue evenly along the groove and place the new strip in position along the first line.

8 Some proprietary laminated floorboards are supplied with a tongue-and-groove piece of plastic for knocking the next boards into place. If yours are not, use a scrap piece of wood to cushion the edge of the board against the blows of the hammer. Work along the boards, making sure they fit together snugly.

Helpful hints

To fit around pipes, mark and cut out a wedge shape from the front of the pipe, trim the wedge to fit around the back of the pipe, then glue and nail in position.

9 Before the excess glue, that will squeeze out as you hammer the boards together, has had time to set, wipe it off with a clean, damp cloth. Once each length across the floor is complete and fitting well, nail it into place.

10 In a kitchen, you will be unlikely to have a floor surface without any kitchen units or cupboards. When you reach the point where you need to cut out a shape, turn the board over as in step 5 and place it against the unit with its end level with the next strip in the line. Use a combination square to mark a line that meets the outside edge of the unit, and extend the line across the board.

11 Keep the new strip in position and use the combination square to measure the depth of the unit from the last laid board. Transfer this depth along the length of the new strip, and mark a cutting line along it. Shade in the waste wood to be cut out.

12 Clamp the strip to your workbench and cut out the waste wood with the fine-tooth crosscut saw or jigsaw. Aim for as accurate a cut as possible, although minor deviations from the line can be hidden with molding. Check the fit against the unit, then apply glue and nail in as before.

Helpful hints

For a wood finish, you can also buy parquet floor squares from hardware stores. These tiles may be self-adhesive, and some have a bitumen base to reinforce the polyethylene layer against dampness.

13 Continue to cut and lay the floorboards, making sure the end-to-end joints are staggered across the whole floor. When you have finished, allow the glue to dry, remove the spacers, and measure the amount of ¾-in. quadrant molding you will need, remembering to add extra for each miter at the corners. Start by mitering and laying the molding along a straight wall, then position long strips and mark their edges.

14 Set the miter saw to 45 degrees and cut the molding. For internal angles such as the corners of the room, the marked line is the outer angle and you cut in from it, while for external angles, such as around units, the marked line is the inner angle and you cut out from it.

15 Check that each strip fits the next, make any necessary adjustments, and nail in place using 1-in. veneer pins. These should be driven in across the deepest part of the molding and emerge at the right angle at the base. Work carefully so you don't damage the floorboards, baseboard, or units.

16 Use a center punch to push the heads below the surface of the molding, fill the holes, and sand them smooth. You can stain the molding to match the floorboards or use a different woodstain for a contrasting effect. Finish by thoroughly cleaning and degreasing the floor and molding, then protect the surface with three or four coats of clear floor varnish, following the manufacturer's instructions.

51

chapter 3
windows

painting a **window**

Painting a window is easy to get right when you do it properly—and just as easy to get wrong if you don't! The vital elements are taking time to prepare the surfaces, and the order of painting the different parts.

Materials

Gloss paint • Undercoat paint (optional) • Primer paint (optional) • Wood putty (optional)

Tools

Utility knife • Straightedge • Fine felt-tip pen • Glass cleaner or methylated spirits (denatured alcohol) • Lint-free cloth

Skill level

Beginner

Time

After preparation 1–2 hours per coat

1   Take down all curtains and window blinds, then
    remove all window hardware—latches, locks, etc.—
    from the window and frame. So you don't lose them,
    put the screws in plastic bags and tape them to their
    hardware piece. Wash the window and frame with
    proprietary degreaser, rinse, and allow to dry.

2   Check the condition of the window and frame. Minor
    patches of rotten or broken wood can be brushed or
    scraped out with a screwdriver or utility knife, but
    large sections may need to be replaced. Fill any gaps
    or scraped areas with wood putty, applying one thin
    layer at a time and allowing each to dry. Only fill
    the hardware screw holes if you are planning to fit
    new pieces.

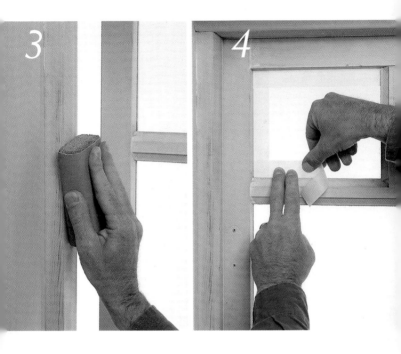

3 Use strips of abrasive paper to rub down any filler until the surface matches the rest of the window or frame. Lightly rub down all other paint to provide a surface for painting. Clean off the dust, and use window cleaner or mineral spirits to thoroughly clean all glass.

4 Cut strips of masking tape to fit the glass where it meets the wood. Press the strips onto the glass, making sure it butts up to the window framing. Overlap the ends at the corners, and press carefully around. This is one of the most important parts of the process, and it's worth taking the time to get it right.

5 If working on bare wood, start by priming it, then apply undercoat when it has dried. For lightly sanded paint, you can go straight to the top coat. Start by painting the crossbars and moldings that hold the glass in the center in the window. We used a 1½-in. brush, but you can use a 1-in. one for small surfaces.

6 Next paint the top and bottom horizontal crossrails. Then apply paint to the vertical hanging stile, the one nearest the hinges. With the window fully open, paint around the edge from the hanging stile to the outer edge, taking care not to get paint on the moving parts of the hinges.

7 Finish the window by painting the other vertical, the meeting stile. If you've been priming or applying undercoat, repeat the order of painting in steps 5–8. Next, paint the frame.

8 Allow the final coat to reach an almost-dry stage, then run a sharp utility knife exactly where the window glass meets the wood, using a straightedge for accuracy. Working from the top corner overlap, remove the tape carefully. Scrape spots of paint off the glass or clean them with mineral spirits while damp. When the paint is completely dry, replace the hardware.

Helpful hints

Don't try to cut corners by using inappropriate paint. There are plenty of combinations available—primer/undercoat, one-coat topcoat—and it pays to read the manufacturer's instructions carefully and follow them.

customizing a
roller blind

Once you've decided a roller blind is what you want for
your kitchen, the next stage is choosing between the
bewildering number of hardware types on the market.
The project model here uses a two-cord mechanism,
available from most stores; the more sophisticated,
spring-loaded models may have more complicated
instructions, but the basic principle is the same.

Materials

Roller-blind kit • Fabric paint

Tools

Screwdriver • Bradawl • Utility knife or scissors •
Straightedge • Pencil • Fine-point, felt-tip pen • Small
hacksaw • Masking tape • Sponge or brush • Abrasive paper •
Carpenter's level • Measuring tape

Skill level

Beginner/Intermediate

Time

2 hours

1 Hold the roller-blind bracket in place, making sure you leave enough room for the mechanism and roller at the top, and mark the screw holes with a bradawl. Check that the holes are level, using a carpenter's level. Make the holes and then screw in the brackets. Check again with the carpenter's level.

2 Measure the exact distance between the bracket ends, then measure and add on the extra amount taken up by the mechanism at both ends—here, this was $9/16$ in. The final measurement is the exact length to which you will cut the cardboard roll.

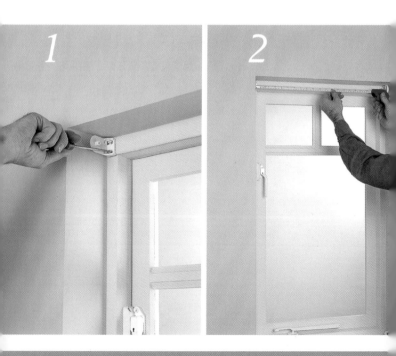

3 Carefully unwind the fabric from the cardboard roll and remove it completely from the end. Drape or fold the fabric with care, to avoid creases. Transfer the measurement from step 2 to the cardboard roll, and cut it to length using a small hacksaw. Gently sand the cut edge level and smooth.

4 Lay the fabric out straight on a surface and remove the plastic rod from the hem at the bottom edge. Reduce the length of the cardboard roll by ¹⁄₁₆ in., and transfer this measurement along the back (window) side of the fabric, using a fine-point, felt-tip pen.

Helpful hints

When fixing the brackets to a horizontal surface above the window, check that the centers are exactly level, using a carpenter's level. If not, insert cardboard or very thin pieces of wood cut to shape inside the higher bracket.

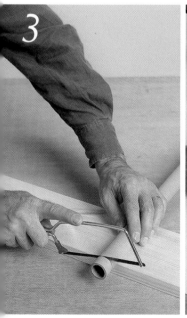

Cut the fabric to width. You can use scissors, but only do this if you are sure of the accuracy of your cutting. A more reliable method is to use a straightedge and utility knife with a sharp blade. Measure the drop in the window recess, add on 6–8 in., and transfer this to the length of the fabric, starting from the hem end. Cut the fabric to length.

Measure the fabric width less ⅛ in., transfer this to the plastic rod, then cut the rod to length with a small hacksaw. Smooth the cut edge with abrasive paper, and put the rod back into the hem to check for fit. When satisfied, remove the rod again.

7 Lay the bottom fabric flat and weight it to hold it in place, then fix two strips of masking tape along the sides on the surface. Measure along the tape from the bottom, matching the marks on each side, then draw lines across the fabric to the marks. Press masking tape onto the fabric along the lines, making sure the edges are firmly in place.

8 Pour some fabric paint into a saucer. Using a brush or sponge, apply the paint to the non-masked areas of fabric. To create the mottled effect shown here, a sponge was pressed on lightly to build up depth of color—you can make the paint more solid, but build it up in the same way.

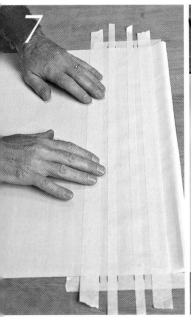

9 Let the fabric paint dry thoroughly and remove the masking tape. Cut a piece of double-sided tape to the width of the fabric, and press it along the length of the cardboard roll, leaving a tiny amount on each side. Strip off the protective backing and press the top end of the fabric exactly onto the tape.

10 Roll up the fabric carefully, making sure the painted side will unroll away from the window. Fit the two side control pieces into the cardboard roll, first by hand to ensure an accurate, straight fit, then using a rubber mallet gently. In the mechanism used in this project, the cords were fitted on the left side.

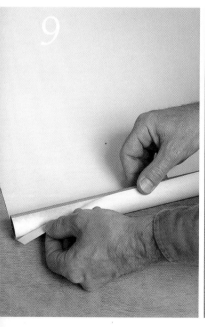

11 Most brackets have different-shape fittings for the control pieces. Making sure the cords are hanging straight down and are untangled, position the control piece in place, then repeat for the other side.

12 On a two-cord mechanism, as here, determine which cord raises the blind. Fit the cord pull to this cord at a convenient height, then make a double knot to hold it in place, and cut off the excess cord with scissors. Lower the blind with the other cord, then repeat with the other cord pull.

Helpful hints

When you fit and lower the blind, it may drop to one side or the other. Remove the roller from the brackets, unwind the blind, and stick a few layers of masking tape onto the roll—left side for a fall to the left, and vice versa.

making an
herb window box

Using fresh herbs in your cooking is always pleasant, and growing your own is even better. This simple, traditional-style window box is designed to take four small or three medium-size plant pots, though you can adapt the dimensions to suit your own window ledge.

Materials (all lumber is softwood unless otherwise stated)

1 piece MDF 21^{11}/$_{16}$ x ¾ x 8⅜ in. • 4 pieces 7¾ x 1¼ x 1¼ in. •
4 pieces 22⅜ x ¼ x 1⅜ in. • 4 pieces 8½ x ¼ x 1⅜ in. •
26 pieces 7 x ¼ x 1¼ in. • ⅜ in. and 1 in. brads • 1½ in. no.
6 screws

Tools

Backsaw or miter saw • Crosscut saw • Sliding bevel •
Square • Screwdriver • Hammer • Drill with pilot and
countersink bits • Center punch • Straightedge • Pencil •
Bradawl • Abrasive paper and cork or foam block • PVA
(white) glue • Wood putty

Skill level

Intermediate

Time

2–3 hours

1 Measure and cut four corner posts to 7¾ in. from
1¼ x 1¼ in. softwood, four front and back rails overlength to 26⅜ in., four side rails overlength to 12½ in.
from ¼ x 1⅜ in. softwood, and 26 uprights to 7 in.
from ¼ x 1¼ in. softwood. If you use a miter saw, set
the blade to a 90-degree angle.

2 On each upright, mark ½ in. from each side across the
top edge, and the same distance down each side
edge, to give 45-degree angles. Draw diagonal lines
between these marks and shade in the waste wood.
Set the miter saw to 45 degrees and cut off the
waste. Repeat for all the uprights.

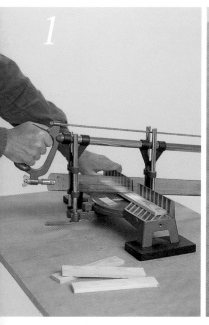

3 Using medium-grade abrasive paper, sand smooth the rough edges of the mitered upright ends.

4 Again using medium-grade abrasive paper, sand a small bevel on each top corner of the corner posts. These bevels can be as pronounced as you like—here, they are enough to take the sharp edges off. You can use abrasive paper wrapped around a sanding block if you prefer.

Helpful hints

Using a miter saw, you can cut two or more pieces of wood at the same time. Make sure that you place the pieces to be cut exactly together.

5 Lay out the four bottom rails, two at 26⅜ in. and two at 12½ in., and mark a line ¼ in. lengthwise above the bottom edge of each rail. This will mark the bottom edge of the uprights.

6 Using a square for accuracy, position one top long rail exactly above a bottom long rail with a gap of 3½ in. between them. Measure and mark 2 in. in from one end on both rails, then place an upright with its outer edge against these marks and its bottom edge on the line drawn in step 5. Apply glue to the rails and nail the upright in place, using ⅜-in. brads. Repeat for all the pairs of rails.

7 Measure and mark ⅝ in. from the inner edge of the first upright, then apply glue and brad the next upright along. Repeat until you have ten uprights along each pair of long rails and three uprights along each pair of side rails. Drive in the brad heads with a center punch, and clean off excess glue as you go along.

8 From the outer edges of the last uprights, mark 1¾ in. vertically across both pairs of long rails, and cut to these lines. On the side pairs of rails, the distance from the outer edges of the uprights is 1½ in. Check that all cut edges are square, and sand them smooth.

Easy home improvements

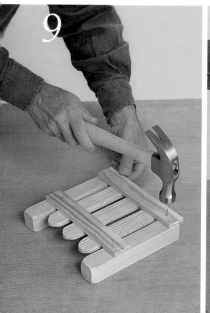

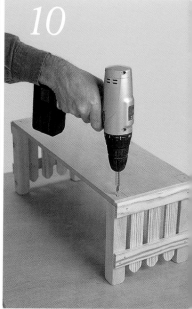

9 To fix the side-rail assemblies to the corner posts, lay two posts flat and position the ends of the rails flush with the outer edges of the posts, with the base of the posts aligned with the line drawn in step 5. Mark the positions, then apply glue and nail in place, using 1-in. brads.

10 Cut the base to 21¹¹⁄₁₆ x 8⅜ in. from ¾ in. MDF, check that the corners are square, and sand smooth. Place one side assembly at the end and mark around the posts. Drill pilot holes, then turn the base over and countersink from the bottom. Apply glue to the bottom of the posts and screw into place.

11 Position the long rail assemblies, checking that the ends of the rails finish flush with the outer edge of the side rails. Apply glue along the edge of the base, replace the assembly and fix the bottom rail using three ½-in. brads. Glue and nail the rail ends to the corner posts, with two brads for each rail end.

12 Use a center punch to drive all brad heads below the surface of the wood. Fill the resulting holes with wood putty, allow to dry, then sand smooth using fine-grade abrasive paper. Give the whole window box a final sanding, then apply primer and, when dry, a top coat.

chapter 4
storage solutions

1. Making a Shaker-style plate rack

2. Making a pot holder

making a Shaker-style
plate rack

This handsome plate display rack has the clean, elegant lines and overall utilitarian simplicity of Shaker furniture. Most original Shaker pieces are made of native American woods such as cherry or maple, but the cost of these is very high so this project used standard softwood that can be painted. For an authentic "period" look, ask your paint-supply store for details of casein or milk paints in traditional colors and hues.

Materials (all lumber is softwood)

• 2 pieces 36 x 1 x 4 in. • 1 piece 28 x 1 x 5 in. • 2 pieces 26 x ¾ x ¾ in. • 2 pieces 26 x ⅝ x 1¼ in. • 2 pieces 24 x 1 x 4 in. • 3 pieces 24 x ¼ x ¼ in. • 1½ in. no. 6 screws • ½ in. brads • 1½ in. brads

Tools

• Crosscut saw • Backsaw • Combination square • ½ in. chisel • Wooden mallet • Straightedge • Pencil • Hammer • Drill with pilot hole and countersink bits • Screwdriver • Abrasive paper and sanding block • PVA (white) glue • Wood putty

Skill level

Intermediate

Time

2–3 hours

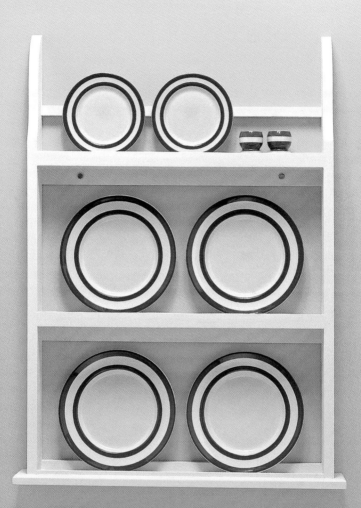

1 Measure and cut the two side pieces to 36 in. from 1 x 4 in. softwood. Smooth off the rough edges and make sure the pieces are identical. Using 1½-in. brads, pin the two pieces exactly together. Draw your chosen pattern for the sides full-size onto a piece of tracing paper, then follow the pattern on the reverse side and trace this pattern onto one of the surfaces. Here, the curve began 9 in. from the top.

2 Clamp the sides securely to the workbench, then cut away the waste wood from the pattern using a power jigsaw. If you are not experienced at cutting curves, it's a good idea to cut just to the outside of the pencil line.

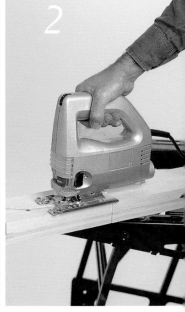

3 Unclamp the sides from the workbench and reclamp them with the cut pattern edge face up. Using medium-grade abrasive paper wrapped around a sanding block, sand the rough edges smooth and identical; if you cut outside the pencil line as in step 2, work methodically until you have the shape you want.

4 Measure, clamp, and cut the top and bottom rails to 26 in. from ¾ x ¾ in. softwood, and the two shelf battens to 26 in. from ⅝ x 1¼ in. softwood, using a crosscut saw. Make sure the pieces are identical lengths, and sand the rough edges smooth.

5 Stand the pinned sides on their front edge (the edge with the pattern cut out). Place the top rail across the sides with its top edge 30 in. from the bottom and mark its edges. Repeat with the upper shelf batten's top edge at 24¾ in. from the bottom, the lower shelf batten's top edge at 12 in. from the bottom and the bottom rail's lower edge flush with the bottom.

6 Use a combination square to mark the positions along one side, then lay the sides flat and use the rails and battens to mark the depth of each component. Turn the sides over and repeat on that surface.

Helpful hints

When using a chisel and mallet, it is best to chop out waste wood using a number of light blows on the chisel rather than one or two hefty ones.

7 Clamp the edges in the workbench with the marked
back edges upward. Using a backsaw held at a slight
angle, cut down the lines of the rails and battens until
you reach the marked depth on the face farthest from
you. Make sure you don't go any farther than this
marked depth. Remove the sides from the workbench
and carefully separate them, then use the rails and
battens to mark a depth line on the two inside faces,
as in step 6.

8 Replace one side in the workbench and saw carefully
to the depth marked on both faces. Repeat for the
other side piece. Lay each side flat and use a utility
knife and straightedge to score along the depth lines.
Turn the wood over and repeat, then do the same on
the other side piece.

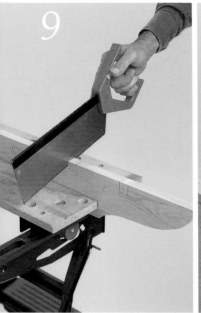

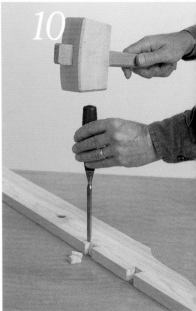

9 Replace one side in the workbench as before and use the backsaw to make one or two further cuts inside the dado joint area for the shelf battens. Again, make sure you cut down to the scored depth line but no farther. Repeat for the other side.

10 Lay one side flat and use a wooden mallet and sharp ½-in. chisel to chop out the waste wood for the dado joints. Start by placing the bevel edge of the chisel blade to the scored depth line with the chisel vertical, then use the mallet to cut the waste out. With the bulk of the waste chopped out, reverse the chisel blade and hold it with the straight end vertical down the scored line. Use hand pressure to clean up the dado housing and get it as square-on as possible. Repeat for all the dado joints on both side pieces.

11 Lay one side piece flat on its inner face, and use a combination square to mark out the position of the two shelves across the outer face. The top edge of the shelf should meet the bottom of the shelf batten, and the bottom edge of the shelf should be 1 in. below the first line. Bring the lines across the front edge, then repeat on the other side piece.

12 Stand the side pieces on their front edges and test-fit the rails and battens into their dado joints. They should be a snug fit, so adjust the dado housings as required and check that they are square. Place each piece in position, drill and countersink two pilot holes at each end for the battens and one for the rails. Remove the rails and battens, apply glue to the dado housings, and drive in 1½-in. no. 6 screws. Wipe off any glue that has squeezed out before it sets.

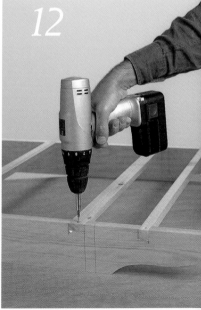

13 Cut the two shelves to 24 in. from 1 x 4 in. softwood, and the base to 28 in. from 1 x 5 in. Clean up the cut edges, check that the lengths are identical, and grip one shelf in the workbench. Use medium-grit abrasive paper wrapped around a sanding block to smooth and round the front edge of the shelf, then remove and repeat with the other one and both edges of the base.

14 Measure and cut the three plate supports to 24 in. from ¼ x ¼ in. softwood. Clean up the cut ends and nail them to the top faces of the shelves and base, ¾ in. from the front edge, using ½-in. brads. The shelf supports run the whole length of the shelves, while the support for the base is set 2 in. from either end.

15 Fit one shelf in place, using the lines across the front of the sides as a guide, and checking the internal angles with a square. Hold in position, then drill and countersink two pilot holes per side. Apply glue to the end of the shelf, insert 1½-in. no. 6 screws, and tighten them. Repeat for the other shelf.

16 Lay the base flat on its bottom face and stand the shelf on it, with an equal overlap on both ends of the sides. Mark the positions of the sides and remove them, then draw guidelines around the base. Drill and countersink two pilot holes through the bottom of the base, position the sides, bradawl through the holes and drive in 1½-in. no. 6 screws. Fill the brad and screw holes with wood putty, sand, and paint with primer and a top coat.

making a
pot holder

Having a separate, free-standing pot holder means you can not only display your pots and pans in the kitchen, but also free up space in cupboards. Once the measuring and marking have been done, constructing the project is relatively straightforward. All the pieces are made from 1 x 1 in. softwood, and you need about 43 ft. in all—the longer the strips you can buy from a lumber yard, the less your materials bill will be.

Materials (all lumber is softwood)

2 pieces 35½ x 1 x 1 in. • 2 pieces 38¾ x 1 x 1 in. •
4 pieces 13½ x 1 x 1 in. • 2 pieces 13¾ x 1 x 1 in. •
22 pieces 12 x 1 x 1 in. • 2 pieces 8⅞ x 1 x 1 in. •
1½ in. brads • 1¼ in. no. 6 screws • 2¼ in. no. 8 screws

Tools

Backsaw or miter saw • Sliding bevel • Square • Screwdriver •
Hammer • Drill with pilot and countersink bits • Straightedge •
Pencil • Bradawl • Abrasive paper and cork or foam block •
PVA (white) glue • Wood putty

Skill level

Intermediate

Time

3–4 hours

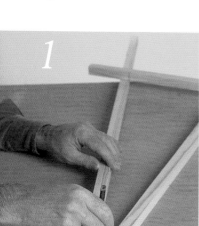

1 Measure and cut the two back (vertical) uprights about 3 in. overlength at the top to 38½ in. Lay one flat, then mark 10 in. up from the bottom edge. Lay a 13¾-in. strip of wood with its bottom edge on this mark, and check that it is square. Mark 10 in. along this new strip from the back edge, then lay a long strip across the others, meeting the upright at 35½ in. at the back.

2 Angle the long strip so its inside edge comes out to the horizontal strip's 10-in. mark. Mark the meeting angle of the uprights across the back upright, then remove the horizontal and front upright and draw a line square across, 1 in. up from the front edge of the angled line. Shade in the waste, cut the top, and repeat on the other back upright.

3 Lay one back upright flat and replace the horizontal and front upright strips—the latter should fit along the cut angle on the back upright to give a straight top. Use a square and straightedge along the bottom of the back upright to mark a line across the front upright. Cut to length, check both bottom edges, and repeat on the other front upright.

4 Lay both back uprights together along their length and measure and mark the positions of the battens across them—the bottom batten's lower edge is 10 in. from the bottom, the middle batten's lower edge is 8¾ in. above this mark, and the top batten's lower edge is another 8¾ in. above that mark. Repeat on the other back upright.

5 Cut all four battens (including the top one) to 13½ in. length, check that both ends are square, and sand the ends smooth. Drill pilot holes at each end, then countersink them. Lay the battens in position across both uprights, making sure the ends are flush with the upright outer edges, then bradawl through the pilot holes, apply glue, and screw in position.

6 Measure and cut 20 slats to 12 in., check that the ends are square, then use abrasive paper and a sanding block to bevel the edges lengthwise. You don't need to make a pronounced bevel, just enough not to catch the bottoms of pots when you put them onto the slats and remove them.

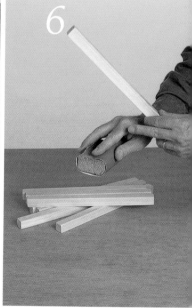

7 Measure and cut the two bottom shelf supports to 13¾ in., the two middle ones to 12 in., and the two top ones to 8⅞ in. Check that they are square and clean up the ends. The back slats on each shelf are 2 in. from the back edge, so mark this on the top edge of the supports, then apply glue and brad this slat in place through the batten.

8 Butt two more slats against the back one, then mark, glue, and brad the second one in place. Repeat for all the slats on all three shelves. The front edges of the shelves will overhang the front slats, so trim the front support edges to length, then sand them flush with the front slat.

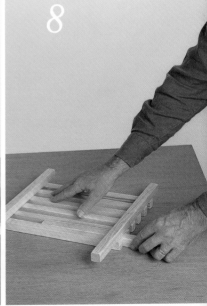

9 Place the bottom shelf in position, with the back edges of the supports fitting onto the bottom batten. Mark the batten for screw holes from below, then drill pilot holes and countersink them. Repeat this process for all three shelves.

10 Hold the shelves in place, and mark through the pilot holes in the battens with a bradawl. Remove the shelf and apply glue to the bottom back edge of each shelf support, then position it and screw into place.

Helpful hints

When fitting the slats, either snip the sharp ends off the brads to prevent them from splitting the wood, or use a tiny drill bit to drill brad pilot holes.

11 Position the top batten at the top of the back uprights and mark, drill, and countersink pilot holes. Bradawl through the holes, then drill pilot holes through the back uprights and bradawl through these into the front uprights. Screw all three pieces together on one side, then repeat for the other side.

12 Make sure the shelves are at right angles to the back uprights, then position the front uprights to the shelf side and drill pilot holes through the uprights. Apply glue to the inner edges of the uprights, then screw in place. Fill all the countersunk holes with wood putty, sand smooth when dry, and finish the pot holder by painting or varnishing it.

chapter 5
repairs

replacing a
cupboard door

As well as fitting new doors as a substitute for ones that have been damaged, replacing kitchen-unit doors is an inexpensive way of giving your kitchen a make-over and a completely new look. Even if you are using the same design and color of door, fitting new handles can ring the changes well.

Materials
Doors • Door handles • Screws

Tools
Screwdriver • Power drill and pilot bit • Pencil • Carpenter's level

Skill level
Beginner

Time
1 hour

1 Unless the old doors were built from solid wood and hung with flush hinges, you will need to use the original "knock-down" hinge hardware, assuming these pieces are not damaged. Support the door or get an assistant to help, and untighten the screws that hold the hinges onto the door. Remove the door.

2 Hold the new door to the hinge mechanism, checking the position of the screw holes. If these don't match, mark the positions on the new door and carefully drill a small pilot hole. Fit the hinge mechanism snugly into the precut recess and screw the door to the hinges.

Helpful hints

If one or more hinges are damaged, or you want to replace them anyway, take off the door first, then unscrew and remove the hinges from the frame. Reassemble in the reverse order and check the fit as described in step 3.

3 The two screws on the hinge mechanism control the distance between the door and frame at the hinge end, and the snugness of the fit at the other end. Working one at a time, loosen each screw and move the door slightly to a new position, then tighten the screw and check the fit of the door to the whole frame. Continue until you are satisfied with the fit.

4 Door handles and knobs come in all shapes, sizes, and materials, but they all need to be screwed or bolted in place. The essential thing here is to measure the positions for the screw or bolt holes accurately—use a carpenter's level as well—then drill the holes and drive in the screws or screw the bolts through and tighten the nuts at the rear of the door.

replacing **sealant**

You may wish to replace old sealant for one of many reasons—it may be discolored or cracked, or it may have contracted or expanded over time. Whatever the cause, the solution comes down to scrupulous preparation, otherwise the problems will start again.

Materials

- Sealant

Tools

Bradawl or old screwdriver • Fine-grade abrasive paper •
Soft brush • Shaping tool • Cloth • Hair dryer

Skill level

Beginner

Time

Under 1 hour

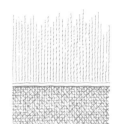

1. Use a bradawl or old, narrow-blade screwdriver to scrape out old sealant. Even if only a small area is affected, it is worth clearing all the sealant along one line, so the result looks like all one piece.

2. Clear away the scraped bits, then fold a small piece of fine-grade abrasive or emery paper, and use this to roughen (key) the surfaces ready for the new sealant. For both this and step 1, work carefully so you don't scratch or chip the wall or work surface.

Helpful hints

If you don't have a soft brush , you can use an old paint-brush, as long as it is completely clean and dry—use a hair dryer to ensure dryness.

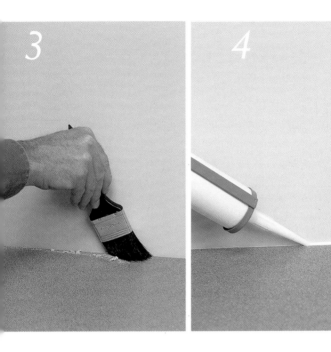

3 Thoroughly sweep out the gap and whole area, using
a soft-bristle brush. You can use a vacuum cleaner as
well. If you are in any doubt that the surfaces are
completely dry, set a hair dryer on hot and play it over
them for a few minutes. Keep the dryer moving.

4 Cut the nozzle of the sealant to a 45-degree angle,
then apply new sealant along the gap, making sure it
is completely filled. Work steadily, and if you have to
pause remove the nozzle from the gap, clean it, and
only then continue. Compress and shape the sealant
with a round-edge tool, and clean up any excess
sealant with a clean, damp cloth immediately.

stencil
templates

Stencilling has been a popular method for applying regular patterns, motifs, and designs to walls for centuries, and many standard stencils are available from art-supply stores. You can also find inspiration from books on interior decoration and folk-art designs, many of which are copyright-free. The ones shown on the following pages are reasonably simple to make—copy them full-size onto blank stencil paper or card (available from the outlets mentioned above), or use a photocopier to enlarge or diminish the size to your own requirements. If you intend to make a number of templates for use along a stretch of wall, make sure you draw and cut them in the same position on each piece of stencil paper or card—that way, you should avoid problems in aligning them exactly on the wall when you have joined them together with adhesive tape.

Materials
• Stencil paper or card • Adhesive tape

Tools
• Pencil or fine-point, felt-tip pen • Utility or hobby knife

Skill level
Beginner

Time
15–25 minutes per stencil

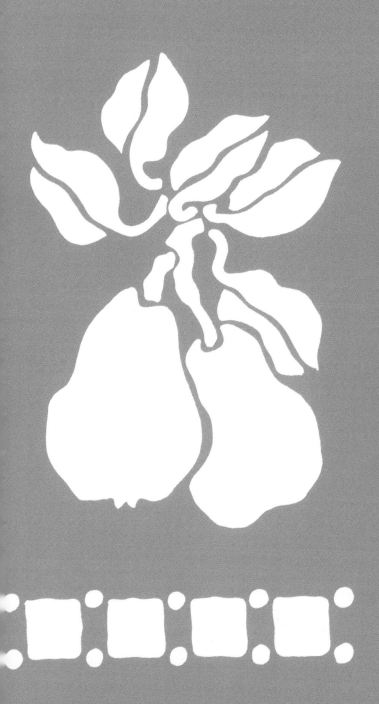

glossary

Batten – a narrow strip of wood; often used to describe such a strip used as a support for other pieces

Bevel – any angle other than a right angle at which two surfaces meet

Butt joint – a simple joint where two pieces of wood meet with no interlocking parts cut in them

Countersink – to cut, usually drill, a hole that allows the head of a screw, nail, or brad to lie below the surface

Crossbar – molded wood separating glass panes

Dado – a shallow, wide groove cut across the grain of a piece of wood; a dado joint is one where a piece of wood is fitted into a dado

Galvanized – screw or nails covered with a protective layer of zinc; used mainly for exterior work

MDF – medium-density fiberboard; a prefabricated material that can be worked like wood

Miter – a joint made by cutting equal angles, usually at 45 degrees to form a right angle in two pieces of wood; cutting such a joint

Pilot hole – a small-diameter hole drilled into wood to act as a guide for a screw thread

Rabbet – a stepped, usually rectangular, recess cut along the edge of a piece of wood as part of a joint

Rail – a horizontal piece of framing in a door or window

Ripping – sawing wood along the grain

Softwood – wood cut from trees, like pine, maple, and cedar, belonging to the botanical group *Gymnospermae*

Stile – a vertical piece of framing in a door or window

Template – a cut-out pattern on paper or cardboard, used to help shape wood

Upright – a vertical piece of wood used in making a frame or carcass

index

Easy home improvements

acknowledgments

All photographs taken by Alistair Hughes, except for:

8/9 Houses & Interiors; 34/35 Simon Upton/ Robert Harding
Syndication; 52/53 Houses & Interiors; 76/77, 96/97 Camera
Press.

Illustrations by Stewart Walton.